ALL TOLEDO

Text, photographs, lay-out and reproduction, entirely designed and created by the Technical Department of EDITORIAL ESCUDO DE ORO, S.A.

Rights of total or partial reproduction and translation reserved.

6th Edition, April 1984

I.S.B.N.

Spanish	84-378-0476-0
English	84-378-0601-1

Dep. Legal B. 14455-1984

editorial **escudo de oro, s.a.** Palaudarias, 26 - Barcelona, 4 - Spain

Impreso en España - Printed in Spain
F.I.S.A. Palaudarias, 26 - Barcelona-4

El Greco saw Toledo enveloped in a blue, cotton-like atmosphere, with angels in its skies. Rilke wrote that Toledo is «a city of Heaven and Earth, for it is in both places simultaneously».

HEBREWS, MOORS AND CHRISTIANS

The traveller reaches Toledo. He contemplates the city, fortified like a castle in her ochre and dusty mountain, gifted with a generous sun, circled and conquered by the river Tajo that passes by obstinately at the hem of her skirt. And the traveller, without a doubt, draws closer to Toledo. He can now make out the severe and geometrical massive structure of the Alcázar, the high and armoured profile of the Cathedral, the city's walls and her portals... And the traveller will instinctively enter Toledo.

One would say, on observing the city from afar, that Toledo is a town in a state of readiness for war, a military village, closed off, impassible. But El Greco painted it in a mystical haze made of dust and sky; like a land incited by cadaverous dreams of glory. Few cities inspire in the traveller as he draws nearer to the city's gates such a tremendous sensation of hermitage. On contemplating the city for the first time, we experience that restless sense of loneliness and isolation that overtakes us as we become more fully acquainted with certain pages in Spain's history. Do not forget that Toledo —as Pérez Galdós wrote— is a complete history of Spain. But we shall not be impressed by the blazonry and walls that have covered the

The blazon displayed on the front of the gate of San Martín portrays the imperial arms, with eagles, of the city of Toledo.

The remains
of the Roman
village, erased
by the passage
of time, are
scant and at
times almost
unrecogni-
zable, like this
drain.

Museum of the Councils and of the Visigothic Culture: this deteriorated VII century piece is obviously not on a par with the splendour of Toledo in the epoch of the great Councils. But history always runs through Toledo leaving a clear print: a matter of life or death.

The Taller del Moro: *this Mudejar decorated earthen jar reminds us that Toledo was the capital of Hebrews, Moors, and Christians.*

sentimental heart of Toledo. Because this city where —inevitably— the traveller has set foot, was in times not so remote the common dwelling place of Hebrews, Moors, and Christians, the place where they learned to live together. Toledo is an unmistakable image of the Middle Ages. However, the Middle Ages in Spain is a history of harmony among communities and of tolerance: The history of three diverse human groups that comprehended one another and lived together until well into the XV century.

From the Roman *Toletum*, a fortified city, capital of the *Carpetania*, there scarcely remain vestiges. However, we shouldn't underestimate the seeds of civilization that these first colonializations left in the gestures and in the soul of the city. Marañón, for example, is of the opinion that Toledo is "more Mediterranean than all of the cities of Greece, of Italy, and of our Eastern shores". Capital of the Gothic monarchy, it was the seat of the famous counsels that etched the polemic tone of Spanish Christianity and which wrote the most important body of juridical procedures of the epoch: the *Fuero Juzgo.* Strolling through Toledo we continue to be assaulted by that lingering image, military and somber, of the ancient capital of the Germanic invaders. But together with this aspect, together with that ar-

Museum of the Councils and of the Visigothic Culture. Remains of Christian origin: this beginning of the Credo carved in stone brings to mind the importance of the Councils of Toledo, in which the most important legal code of the epoch was drawn up.

cheological stamp of the Gothic domination, we still come upon the unmistakable remains of the Toledo of the Arabs and of the Hebrews. From the date of the Reconquest, when Alphonso VI reclaimed the city from the Moors in 1085, Toledo was transformed into the "imperial city". It is said that Charles V felt more like an emperor when he set foot upon the stairs of the Alcázar. But it was also in Toledo where that heroic, popular revolution of the *comuneros* took root and which jeopardized the imperial authority of the House of Austria. The village of Toledo was following, step by step, that unsure thread of Spain's history that culminated in tragedy with the defeat of the Invincible. The empire was shipwrecked in the Atlantic, and in the Mediterranean, and also in the Caribbean. And "imperial Toledo", ruined in her transparent sky or on its dusty hill, was converted into a humble city that worked patiently in the process of regeneration and in the art of her age-old industry of firearms. But history does not abandon Toledo; and everything that the city exposes to the sun of her squares and her balconies is impregnated with that indelible sense of history that traces noble blazons even on the clothing hung out to dry on the homes of Toledo. Toledo appears to be a military city; it is a somber eagle, the heart of Spain.

Toledo, on a stretch of land cut by the Tajo, tempered by centuries of history, has a scattered, horizontal look interrupted only by the huge mass of the Cathedral and that of the Alcázar.

A BASTION ON THE RIVER TAJO: Castles, walls, gates and bridges of Toledo.

The river Tajo, incisive and curving, surrounds Toledo like a cutlass. Participant in the tempering of arms and characters, forger of empires and rolling clouds of mist, the Tajo is the enigma of Toledo. The traveller that approaches the city and contemplates it upright in the midst of the countryside, cannot avoid being overcome by a sense of helplessness before the striking appearance, heroic and somber, of the square of the city. Fortified towers, walls and portals place themselves in his path, as if they were there to obstruct his way. So overwhelming is the spirit of the city that even the distant smell of forgings and temperings, of swords and halberds, penetrates into the pores and imagination of the traveller.

Of river and wall enshrouded,
exemplary of heroic majesty.

As the verses of Lope de Vega indicate, Toledo appears in the eyes of the visitor like a bulwark or impregnable bastion. But it is necessary to get closer in order to discover these bridges that are the vanguard of Toledo's hospitality.

The bridge of Alcántara is defended and escorted by two towers; one is baroque, from the XVIII century, and the other, with a double door and portcullis, was built in 1217. Although restored, it is probably the most ancient bridge.

The bridge of San Martín, built at the foot of San Juan de los Reyes church, was designed by the architect Arévalo.

The castle of San Servando stands opposite the bridge of Alcántara.

"Old bridge of Alcántara over the harmonious Tajo river! Eternal muse of the river that joins in its torrent the voice of Garcilaso, the divine, to an intriguing, melancholy song of sweet Portugal." Yes! Brilliant and melancholy —as suggested by the verses of Emilio Carrere— Toledo displays that poetic and tender aspect of its personality each and every time that her bridges are crossed.

Only two bridges, that of Alcántara and San Martín, cross the Tajo river. The Alcántara bridge was probably the only access to Toledo during the greater part of the Middle Ages. The present construction pertains to Arabic workmanship. The bridge of San Martín, more modern, crosses the Tajo in a powerful span of three arcades. It is said that the architect Arévalo, its builder, did not consider the original design to be sufficiently safe and he was afraid that, on withdrawing the scaffolding, the work would collapse. His wife set fire to the forms that supported the bridge during the night so that there would then exist a pretext for its reconstruction.

But if the bridges are the vanguard of Toledo's hospitality, the gates or portals should draw us definitely into this mysterious, three-dimensional world —Hebrew, Moor, and Christian, as will be remembered— of the town. Toledo, is circumspect

The bridge of San Martín provides access to Toledo by means of a round arch that is ennobled with a coat of arms.

beauty in a cloister setting that shields itself from the eyes of those who wish to catch a glimpse of its existence. Having overcome the severe cutlass that is the Tajo river we find ourselves now confronted by the stern belt of her walls. The traveller must pass through the door with the fortified tower of the Sun, through the two portals —Old and New— of Bisagra, throught the doors of the Cambrón or Valmardón. Because the doors of Toledo, with their arches and blazons, should always be viewed both from outside and from within, coming and going. The bridges can be contemplated from afar; they are roads, but they could as well be arches suspended over the Tajo to support this stone fortress. The doors should be viewed from nearby and crossed in both directions. It is of no importance if we choose the Old door of Bisagra, where the Cid entered Toledo and also Alphonso VI, or the door of the Cambrón with its gigantic shield of the town. Upon crossing any of them, the traveller is endowed with that baptism of intimacy and sober shadows that will help him to understand Toledo.

The baroque gate of Alcántara also has the coat of arms of Toledo carved on its front.

The Puerta del Sol, *a beautiful example of Mudejar craftsmanship, erected in the XIV century. It is one of the most representative monuments of Toledo's architecture.*

The Puerta Nueva de Bisagra, with its gigantic imperial coat of arms, built in 1550; perhaps on the ruins of an old Arabic gate.

The Puerta Antigua de Bisagra, also called that of Alfonso VI because it was perhaps used by that monarch to enter the town in 1085.

The gate of Alfonso VI presents a wide diversity of elements, corresponding to its venerable history.

TOLEDO, SPIRITUAL CAPITAL OF SPAIN

Toledo isn't, like Madrid, the official centre of Spain. Philip II, who had a surveyor's as well as a geometric concept of the monarchy, didn't accept it as the capital of the empire. Neither does it stand out for long-kept and pure independence that benefitted Valladolid, enabling it to serve as capital city in an era when the Catholic King and Queen wished to find the unity of Spain in an unswerving justification, free of Hebrew or Moorish influences. Toledo, on the other hand, is a city open to all races, to all cults. It is the site where all invaders came together, and where, in miniature, are heaped together all of the ingredients pertinent to Spain's history. It would be difficult to look for racial or geometric pureness in the soul of Toledo. Toledo is tolerance, coexistence, acceptance. Here is the essence of its hospitality, its air of comprehension. Here also is to be found an explanation for its undefeatable character so representative of the conscience of Spain; in Toledo the main lines of Spanish history and thought come together; in Toledo Spain's most attractive and forgotten biography of mutual understanding amongst divergent cultures and a spirit of communication has been forged. Scene of the most notable counsels and assemblies of the Church since the year 400, Toledo is the primated

Domingo de Céspedes, Felipe Vigarny and Berruguete produced the figures and sculptures of the choir of Toledo Cathedral. Vicente Salinas made the lectern, incorporating an eagle.

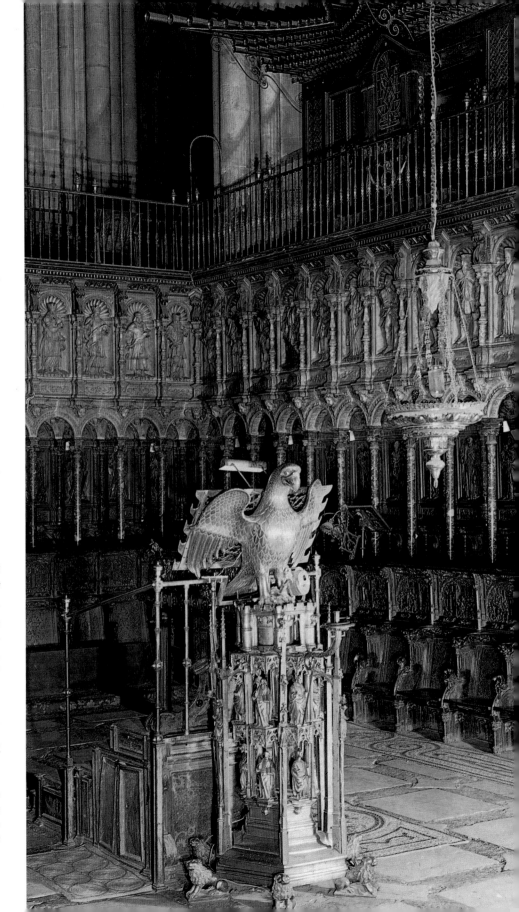

The western
façade, the
main one of
Toledo
Cathedral,
was begun in
the XV
century and
completed in
the following
century. The
tower has a
height of 90
metres and
the cupola
was designed
by the son of
El Greco.

The door of
the Lions was
built in the
XVI century
by the
Flemish
architect
Annequín
Egas, and
adorned by
Juan Alemán.
It owes its
name to the
lions that top
off the six
columns
supporting the
railing.

The interior of the Cathedral consists of a nave and four large aisles. The nave is forty metres high.

seat of Spanish Catholicism. That long —and sometimes compacted— history of Christian fidelity has left its mark on a pleasing succession of churches, chapels, and diminutive sanctuaries that enshrine, within their towers and merciful silence, our preoccupied stroll along Toledo's streets. From the narrow city lanes of the old quarter to the spacious fields of the lowlands, Toledo unravels these indisputable credentials of Christian history: Church bells that toll or are now mute, clipped towers or those that can count only scant days of existence, crumbling cloisters or those still inhabited by the legend of the monk, sleeping gardens or those with flowers reminiscent of a sacred meditation...

But if Toledo is —in its own right— the primated seat of Hispanic Catholicism, it could also be the primated synagogue of Spanish Hebrew rites, the Jerusalem of the West, the old and lost refuge of a people possessed by a scorned soul. How similar is the heart of Toledo to that fateful utterance pronounced on the ghetto's lips! How inhabited is the heart of Toledo with plaintive legends of the errant Jew!

There's no doubt: Toledo was in the XI, XII and XIII centuries, the Jerusalem of Spanish Jews. Even the toponymy of Toledo —those towns with an ancient and Biblical ring to their names: Maqueda, Escalona, Yepes— remind us of the toponymy of Palestine: Maqueda, Askalon, Yoppe... Her streets were for centuries the mirror and calendar of Hispanic politics; at times open to commerce, to art, and to humanities; other times devasted by struggles. The city's lanes were also the turning point of Spain's history: Today dyed with lime and light, tomorrow dyed with blood. The genetic aptitude of the Jews for the Arts and Mysticism found its support in Spain's best monarchs: Abderramán III, Ferdinand III, Alphonso X, Pedro I... Among the citizens of Toledo were Salomón Abenzachel, the novelist; Aben Ezra, versist, poet, philosopher and wanderer; and, above all, Judá Haleví, the poet of the *Siónidas,* the Camoens or Tassa of Hebrew literature, that restless and troubled wiseman who —according to Heine— carried a kiss of God upon his soul. The mixture of languages and cultures was so evident in the Toledo of those times that Judá Haleví was called "the Castillian". Menéndez Pelayo considers him to be the first writer known in the Castillian language. But if Judá Haleví can be considered a poet in three languages Ferdinand III also deserved the designation, "emperor of men of three religions".

The White Virgin, carved in alabaster, is a masterpiece of XII century French art: a tender, indulgent image of maternity, an innocent and archaic concept of sculpture.

The harmony of the nave and aisles, and the fine smoothness of the columns fuse with the detail work of the screens or with the delicate ornamentation of the walls.

The stained-glass windows, together with the Transparente, are the key to the secret of light and shadows that epitomizes Toledo Cathedral.

Men of three religions —of three worlds, in truth— lived together in Toledo. Men of three religions, of three worlds, of three distinct languages, converted Toledo into the indisputable spiritual capital of Spain. Because this city that we see today with its soul scarcely inhabited by the Tajo river, and memories of its heraldic routing, was a university and sanctuary for people who wrote and prayed in three different languages: the Christian oration of love for God; the Jewish prostration before the forgiveness of God; the Moorish supplication for the joy of God.

THE CATHEDRAL

The Cathedral, or the conversion of the word into space; the transformation into a tower of the hands clasped in prayer; the sign in stone of the faith of men. Without a doubt, the traveller has come upon the Cathedral without having planned to do so; its piercing tower has been visible scores of times to the traveller, beckoning him from any corner. And now, having at last arrived at its foundation, it is worth our while to contemplate it. Constructed upon the site of the ancient, primate church of Recaredo, the present structure was begun during the reign of Ferdinand III. During its one hundred and sixty years, the best architects, masons, and masters in *jometría* of Spain and of Europe, dedicated themselves to its con-

The light filtered through the stained glass windows breaks unexpectedly into this architectonic manifestation of the Transparente; *a shimmer of sunlight in the midst of the shadows, a baroque delirium of images set in a display of harmony.*

25

The choir-stalls, which are perhaps the most important example of the Castilian Renaissance style; the upper part was carved by Berruguete.

struction: Pedro Pérez, Annequín Egas, Joaquín of Utrecht, Alberto of Holland, etc. Seen from the outside, in the confined space that the growth of the town has left behind, the Cathedral of Toledo lacks perhaps the sober impression made by other great Gothic churches in Spain and Europe. It doesn't share the lucid play of arches characteristic of Notre Dame, for example, nor the reviling façade of the towers of Burgos. But one must go within; everything in Toledo needs to be penetrated, fathomed, borne of an inquisitive mind. The attractions of Toledo have —perhaps due to Arabic

The capitular hall is the culminating work of Juan de Borgoña, who painted the frescoes on the walls.

atavism— a very special purity that induces them to close within themselves. This isn't a city of façades or large, exterior, poster-like sights; it isn't like Heidelberg or Berne, a town of busy streets brandished with flowers. Toledo is a town of interiors, of patios and cloisters and sanctuaries, inhabited in the profoundest depths of its heart to such an extent that it has its back to the street. And to confirm even more this passionate psycho-analysis of the soul of Toledo we only have to enter its Cathedral. Few churches in the world can show such a complete range and pureness of cut-glass windows; all colours imaginable, from the deepest red to the lightest blue, an array of pictures and a display of forms. There's a floating garden, a tranparent and flying museum, touching the very air of Toledo's Cathedral. For a moment the surprised traveller would imagine that he is gazing at the walls of a crystal and porcelain Mosque that dots the hills about Istambul.

And if we look in depth at the theme of this painted window we will be able to discern immediately the motifs of Christian iconography. More than seven hundred leaded window panes. A whole esthetic of circumspect beauty: eyes that are not for seeing but for ushering into the spirit the multicoloured morning sunlight. This is what is important in Toledo: the inner

The Virgen del Sagrario is the most venerated image in Toledo and the patron saint of the city. The Romanesque image is of silver.

The cloister, adorned with frescoes by Bayeu and Maella, has Gothic lines. It is built in the same place where the famous market of the Jewish quarter was to be found.

world. This is what stands out in Toledo's Cathedral: the cut-glass windows, the sacristy, the transparent nature of it all, the choir... Even the doors —those extraordinary Gothic portals of Lions, with their iron latticework and forest of statues, or the imposing ogival of Foregiveness— disappear from our memory as soon as we enter within the enclosure. However, perhaps with too much humility, the chapel that guards the monumental tabernacle that Henry of Arfe had made in 1517 has been called the chapel of Treasures. Seventeen arrobas of jewels inside of this other treasure the Cathedral itself. Everywhere the affluence of this artistic treasure beckons to us: in the chapel of the Adoration, an altar attributed to Juan of Borgoña; in the chapel of San Eugenio, the sepulchre of the bishop Castillo, a work by Covarrubias; the Mozarabic chapel traced by Egas; the chapel of Santa Lucía with a figure of Saint John attributed to Ribera; that of Santa Ana with an altar by Gil of Siloé; the Capitular Hall, where Juan of Borgoña left the portrait of the prelates of Toledo, from San Eugenio, to Cisneros; Carducci, Jordán, Rubens, Reni, and —why not— El Greco, the best European painters have left their mark even in

The monstrance by Enrique de Arfe is the pride of the Cathedral's treasures. It is made of solid silver, gold and precious stones. It weighs 195 kilos and includes 5,600 pieces.

In the Vestry of the Cathedral, an authentic museum of paintings with works by Rubens, Bellini, Reni, etc., this magnificent portrait of Paulo III, by Titian, is exhibited.

The Expolio de Cristo, *by El Greco, presides over the main altar of the sacristy.*

the most modest of the chapels of the Cathedral. But perhaps —speaking without prejudice— the culminating movement of this sympnony of forms is the *Transparente*. Narciso Tomé, its creator, has interpreted here, in a delirium of reliefs, foreshortenings and twists, the entire *allegro vivace* of the baroque style. And, suddenly, in the midst of this ascensional ecstasy, the broken movement of the arch... But the *Transparente* has to be viewed in this fashion: against the light, the eyes wounded by this unexpected on-rush of sun that descends upon the arches to the very floor, polishing the foreshortenings, highlighting the unevenness. The architecture has reached this site —as in the interior of Santa Sofía, and as in the façades of the Mosques of Solimán or Taj Mahal— attaining what Eugenio D'Ors called the culmination of spatial art; the "forms that have weight" of the Gothic have transformed themselves into "forms that soar", pertinent to the baroque style. The *Transparente* is, without a doubt, the most daring ascensional attempt of the Cathedral, a more energetic effort than the ogive or pointed arch, even more brave that the tower. The *Transparente,* with its mystical delirium, also has something of those verses of Judá Haleví that sing in burning words to God who created the world.

The Cathedral Vestry includes a large collection of dalmatics, embroidered chasubles and miters. Some items date as far as five centuries back.

This XIII century French miniature is from the Bible that S Louis, King of France, gave to Fernando III. The three volumes, profusely painted in miniature, are kept in the Cathedral Vestry.

In the past travellers spoke of the beauty of the Cathedral on moonlit nights. Today, thanks to the resources of modern technology, we can view it illuminated by lights that are perhaps less romantic but more impressive.

The first archbishop's palace was built by Cardinal Ximenez de Rada. Cardinal Tavera ordered another main door and, later, Cardinal Lorenzana rebuilt the façade.

What carriage will ascend to your House,
inhabitant of the after-life?
What word has been imprisoned with your letters?...
What heart could clothe you
with your own wings?
What eyes could reach
your pinnacle?

With half-closed and wounded eyes, with the heart lost in an impossible flight of wings and pointed structures, replete the carriage of thoughts, where withall the traveller should proceed on with his journey through the temples of Toledo, through the landmarks of this triple and enigmatic spirituality that is the essence of Toledo. Cathedral, Christian oration exemplifying love of God, is now behind us. Leaving to one side the Archbishop's Palace, with its notable Library, we continue our journey. The synagogues, the Jewish supplication imploring God.

The beautiful Mudejar tower of Santo Tomé thrusts its austere, stately silhouette into the clear sky of Toledo.

The synagogue of El Tránsito was erected by the opulent secretary of Peter the Cruel, Samuel Leví. In accordance with Hebrew religious sentiment, no testimony of its importance is manifested in the façade.

Interior of the church of San Román. Alfonso VIII was proclaimed King of Castile at the foot of its tower.

SANTA MARIA LA BLANCA

Of all the synagogues that were to be found in Toledo during the centuries of Jewish splendour, Santa María la Blanca was one of the few that attained the status of a synagogue of the highest order. Although the date of its construction cannot be determined exactly, it can be assumed to pertain to the epoch of Alphonso VIII because of its style. Santa María la Blanca does justice to its name: it is white, of a candid and fresh whiteness, starched and virgin-like. The white Santa María suggests to the imagination of the traveller an innocent liturgy of weddings and coquettish morning prayers, a distracted conscience. The hand that designed it and chose its colour, without a doubt knew perfectly the Arab-Andalusian language interpreted by the sun written on its walls: the morning sunshine that turns streets a bluish hue, the reflection of dusk that converts the light of day into an orange-coloured tone. It is said that the builders of the synagogue were people that had learned in that wretched sun-drenched Northafrican desert the movement of light in open spaces. The synagogue of Santa María retains an evident similarity with the interior of the Kuttubya: that white treasure that those people left on the red-

The synagogue of Santa María la Blanca is without a doubt inspired by the Almohade style. Historical chance has accorded it many functions: synagogue, Christian church, home for repentant women, barracks and warehouse.

dened streets of Marraquech. Even while Jewish, quite clearly Jewish, in the starry ornamentation of the walls, Santa María la Blanca has something of orange blossoms and African Mosques, a remote optimism of an oasis and a milky texture that blends more naturally with Mohammedan sensuality than with the volcanic God of Sinai.

The monastery of San Juan de los Reyes was conceived by Juan Guas who, daringly fusing diverse architectonic elements, here defined the so-called «style of Isabel».

THE SYNAGOGUE OF EL TRANSITO

Here quite definitely we have the true Hebrew spirit, in the synagogue of El Tránsito; here, the Jewish prostration in supplication of forgiveness for sins; here, the Easter sacrifice and the wandering melancholy of the promised land. In spite of the white enchantment of the plaster that covers its walls, the synagogue of el Tránsito has a distant gesture of lonliness, a mysterious profoundness in the work of its roof. Perhaps there is also a sense of fortress in its basic structure: "This is the fortress of perfect letters", a chant inscribed on its walls. A stone tabernacle for an athletic and mighty God,

The lower gallery of the cloister of San Juan de los Reyes looks out upon a well-kept garden that smells of orange blossoms and oranges. The arches and ornamentation of the pillars are in a flamboyant Gothic style.

the synagogue of El Tránsito was
built by the wealthy Samuel Haleví,
treasurer of Peter the Cruel. Contemplating the oppulent ornamentation of its walls, that timid and
meek play of lyric tones with jealous
overtones, of the plaster with stone,
of Gothic with Mozarabic, one
would think that the well-to-do Haleví —the most powerful man in Toledo— wanted to build a palace to
God here so that he would not
keep his word as pronounced by
David: "I live in a palace and the
coffer of Our Lord lies in a meager
tent."

SAN JUAN DE LOS REYES

If the Cathedral or the synagogue
are a reflection of the intimacy of
Toledo that covers with modest façades the luxury of their interiors,
San Juan de los Reyes is on the
other hand a presumptious triumph
of glitter and pageantry. Built by
the Catholic King and Queen as a
mark of victory, it has been conceived for the most part with an
esthetic nobility and sense of
triumph. More than two-hundred
stonecutters worked on its construction. Is is considered as a culmination of the style of the Catholic Queen, Isabel; it is the symbol in terms of a structure, of a
war-like and martial era, aquiline
and stately. It is the symbol of that
other Toledo, imperial and inured
to war that had intimidated us upon
approaching the city.

*The Cristo de la Vega, with His right
hand separated from the cross as if He
were swearing an oath, inspired Zorrilla
to state: «A good judge is a better
witness».*

That Toledo, with the face of an eagle that encloses a tender heart within its outstretched wings. San Juan de los Reyes, in its haughty triumph of blazons and eagles, also hides the solitary and charitable heart of its cloister. Is the traveller tempted to initiate in this corner, in this sweet refuge of orange and ogive, a personal meditation on this history that surrounds him?

OTHER TEMPLES OF TOLEDO: Santiago del Arrabal, Christ of La Vega, Christ of La Luz...

We have already looked out from the large balconies of the spirituality of Toledo: the Cathedral, Santa María la Blanca, Our Lady of El Tránsito, San Juan de los Reyes. But undoubtedly this small meditation in the cloister of San Juan de los Reyes —that small moment of truth that we experienced in its garden of ogives— has prompted us to penetrate deeper into the hidden corners of the soul of Toledo.

There still remains a romantic and humble aspect of Toledo that we can view by following the ardous itinerary of its smaller churches.

The convent of Santo Domingo el Real, with its curious amalgamation of styles, is related to the biography of Peter the Cruel. His lover and his daughter, María of Castile, were prioresses of this convent.

The Mudejar church of Santiago del Arrabal was probably built during the reign of Alfonso VI and re-constructed towards the middle of the XIII century.

We can still go up to Santiago del Arrabal, the Mudéjar church that preserves more jealously the characteristics of its style. We can still reach the old Basilica of Santa Leocadia, popularly known by the name of the church of Christ of la Vega. The green plain and its cypress trees, the endless plain and the small, homely church. The plain and the unkempt Christ, with a hand ripped from the nail and pressed against his forehead, who —according to the legend— has just pronounced the words of a terrible judgement: "I am a witness." The church of Christ of la Vega has its finest hour: The moment of dusk, "that time —writes Becquer— when the sun disappears and the presaging wind of the night extends its humid wings over the waves of the river." The visits to be made are innumerable along this journey through the humble corners of Toledo's spirituality: the hermitage of Christ of la Vega, an ancient Mosque where it is said that king Alphonso left his coat-of-arms when Toledo was taken; Santo Domingo the Ancient and Santo Tomé, united as they are to the life of El Greco...

The church of el Cristo de la Luz was a mosque until the time of the Reconquest. It was here that Alfonso VI heard his first mass upon entering Toledo.

The richness of Toledo's art can be noted at times in the smallest details of the architecture: for example, in the capitals of the columns.

The temples of San Bartolomé and that of the Concepción Francisca, can serve to end this visit to the churches that were once Mosques. And among the Mozarabic churches —aside from the hermitage of the Christ of la Luz, a notable example of the early architecture of el Andalus— we should not overlook the churches of Santa Eulalia and San Sebastián. This latter one still preserves the remains of its murals, that have suffered wear with age, as well as due to the restorations that were practised in the past.

From Zocodover to the plain, from the heights of San Juan de los Reyes to the shores of the Tajo, the traveller has journeyed through the sanctuaries of Toledo's spirituality; he has paid homage to Toledo with the dust and tiredness of his feet, which is akin to all of the old art capitals, demanding of the pilgrim that he launch himself upon its many streets: A tiring tribute that so many times we have paid in Florence, in Rome, in Athens, in Granada, in Avila... Tired and dust-trodden feet. The traveller carries on his feet the trace and testimony of his closeness to the inscrutable and remote conscience of Toledo, the spiritual capital of Spain.

Vaults of Gothic lines crown the naves of the ancient mosque of el Cristo de la Luz, supported on horseshoe-shaped arches that are uplifted in turn by marble columns that end in Visigothic capitals.

The house of El Greco is to be found on the same spot that was once the site of the lavish palace of Samuel Leví. The furnishings provide an image characteristic of XVI century Toledan noblemen's houses.

El Greco, although born outside Spain, came to identify himself with the spirit of Toledo to the extent that he conceived his best work in this town.

EL GRECO AND TOLEDO

But we are viewing Toledo too much from the ground. And this ant-like perspective, almost microscopic, could deceive us and deprive us of one of the most prominent enchantments of the city: its atmosphere. Undoubtedly there exists a link between Toledo and its heavens, between the city and its sky. Any detail at all acquires in the atmosphere of Toledo a transcendental permanence. Perhaps no one has gone so far as El Greco in interpreting this mystical air and hue. El Greco is Toledo's artist. Even the corpselike spirit of its colours, even the deformed and anguished tension of his paintings, has something of this desperate and profound desire for redemption that continues to imbue the air of Toledo. "Something similar to the Toledo of yesteryear —writes Cossío, referring to the *Burial of the Count of Orgaz*— a flourishing life that comes to an end; an intense spirituality, consummated." This mysterious and melancholy world of Toledo is also present in the physionomy of personalities like El Greco; it is in the figure of San Ildefonso; in the tearful gaze of San Pedro; and it's in the eyes of the noblemen that attend the burial of Orgaz in their rôle as participants in his death, as companions in this terrible event, inevitable and representing the final hour of history itself.

A detail of The Burial of the Count of Orgaz.

The Burial of the Count of Orgaz *is one of the masterpieces of El Greco. The painter received 1,200 ducats for having painted it.*

The Hospital de San Juan Bautista was built by Cardinal Tavera and today it is known by the name of its builder. Albeit adulterated by successive retouching, its façade is of stately Renaissance lines.

El Greco's studio, the evocative corner where the artist came face to face with the apparitions of his conscience. On the easel is one of the clearest samples of his painting: Saint Peter.

THE MUSEUMS

Toledo isn't a city of museums. Few cities of the world continue to exude so much life, to be so whole, so rebellious towards showcases and gaudy displays. It could be said that history has penetrated into its sheltered corners quite completely, without hesitating for an instant: a matter of life or death. Things in Toledo don't share that disturbing alchemy present in the Egyptian desert where corpses are mummified, where the dead are eternalized in an unpleasantly comfortable posture in the tomb. History in Toledo has no more and no less than two focal points: Live forever or disappear forever. "What doesn't kill me —commented a philosopher— strengthens me." The same could be said of Toledo, because this Castillian town is, in a certain fashion, a challenge launched against history. Toledo —if we can come to define it— is "a way of life in time". Its museums can't be, and therefore aren't, an exhibition that's more or less interesting of ancient marvels. These remnants of the past that we have no choice but to venerate in cities decimated by the hands of time, do not demand of us any tribute in terms of idolatry in Toledo. Even the buildings themselves that the

The Hospital de Tavera retains, in its decoration and in its furnishings, the characteristics of the stately Castilian manor house of the XVII century.

city has set aside for museums don't have much in the way of archives of history; they are, instead, homes, palaces, refuges still inhabited by a breath of life. The paintings are there, hung on the walls, stationed in the same corner of the dining room where they were always to be found. The books continue to rest in the library, as if the chrism hand of the friar could still reach out each day to leaf through them with gentleness. The mausoleums have not allowed their dead to be whisked away... To visit Toledo's museums is to open a little bit the doors of the hospitality of its history.

THE HOSPITAL OF TAVERA

In the Hospital of Tavera the traveller will feel like a guest and a companion of history. This hospital is known by the people of Toledo by the more familiar name of Hospital of Afuera. It was built, during the reign of Charles I, by the archbishop of Toledo, Juan Pardo de Tavera. The monarch held in such high esteem this statesman that, on hearing of his death is quoted as exclaiming: "Nothing can serve to compensate for me the loss of this ancient figure who conserved peace within my kingdom with his staff."

The Hospital of Tavera is unfinished. None of the architects who worked successively on it (Bartolomé Bustamante, Alonso de Covarrubias, Hernán González de Lara, the Vergara family), was able to finalize the work. Despite this, the Hospital can be included in the most critical showcase of Spanish Renaissance works. In the austere geometry of its façade, in the orderly arrangment of its stonework, in every detail of its architecture, the Hospital has a sense, rather severe, of Spanish Renaissance works. Don't forget that it represents a period characterized by great solidity and responsibility in the history of Spain. The Spanish Renaissance could not be, as occurred with the Italian, a *gaia* adventure in Humanitarianism. The Spanish Court was not only, as other courts or European republics, an optimistic centre of love and pleasantries. The policy of the Spanish empire, that had made efforts to imbue its powers with a sense of morality rather than concede to purely economic motivations, had to express itself in a Cartesian architectural form, austere and, to a certain extent as well, innocent. All of the characteristics, so interesting as they are, come together in the

The Sacred Family *painted by Tintoretto —with a masterly sense of rhythm— is only a small example of the artistic treasures that are to be found in the Hospital de Tavera.*

The delicate lines in the face of this madonna do not seem to spring from human effort, but rather to be a spontaneous stroke of El Greco's genius upon the canvas.

huge mass enclosure of the Hospital of Tavera. Its forms are severe, but at the same time there exists in its gesture, an air of innocence, of a monarchy that trusted more in the historical power of the nobility than in economic forces. But the sagacious passing of time was busy in populating the Hospital of Tavera with other, more noble treasures than those of a handsome façade. Beginning with the patios of a diaphanous and airy design, the entire interior of the palace is a museum of history and art. The church, behind its façade of marble from Carrara, also hides two master works of art pertaining to the Spanish Renaissance: a main altar, work of El Greco, and the carved sepulchre of Cardinal Tavera —who was well-advanced in years— done by Alonso Berruguete. Perhaps in no other work of his did the sculptor attain that merciful and naked vision of death, that tenderness that is almost sarcastic, of the figures that surround the mausoleum. No sign whatsoever of rebelliousness in the gestures; simply an unperturbed and humble resignation.

The Hospital de Tavera houses a magnificent collection of El Greco's works: the Holy Family, Saint Peter, *the* Baptism of Christ, *and the* Portrait of Cardinal Tavera.

Now we move into the interior of the palace; in each of its halls, in each canvas hung on its walls, an authentic biography of Spain's history awaits us. Precisely that biographical concept of the museum of Toledo that is so natural. The Hospital of Tavera doesn't house a mere collection of the most universal artists: Carreño, Caravaggio, Sánchez Coello, Ribera, Tintoretto, Zubarán... but rather it includes them as personalities that epitomize a biography, surprised in a moment of privacy by the genius of the painter; many of the great figures of Spanish history people the walls of the Hospital. Here we are to meet Antonio Pérez, the disturbing secretary of Philip II. Further on we come across Charles V or Isabel Clara Eugenia, and in another corner, the Duke of Medinaceli, the Duchess of Feria and the Marquis of Nava. And, inevitable in any sampling of art in Toledo, El Greco...; El Greco, in the most athletic, tense hour, and anguished moment of his art, of his incredibly stylized figures, in the flash of eyes turned upwards, pushed by asymmetrical winds; El Greco of the *Baptism of Christ*.

But we have already mentioned that the Hospital of Tavera is something more .than a museum. It is a home, in the same way as the Museum of El Greco is a house, and so named.

Another of the gems of the Hospital de Tavera: this Portrait of the Duke of Medinaceli, *still a child, painted by Zurbarán.*

The plateresque façade of the Hospital de Santa Cruz looks like the work of a goldsmith. Cardinal González de Mendoza commissioned Enrique Egas to construct the building.

The Hospital de Santa Cruz now houses, beneath its splendid panelled ceilings, the most important collections of the Museum of Santa Cruz.

The traveller doesn't lose sight of the attractive view of the furnishings that surround him as he journeys through the halls of the Hospital of Tavera: the rugs, gilt and painted desks, large chests, libraries, those objects that make us feel like fortunate guests in this common house that has been furnished, century after century, by the figures and treasures of Spain's history.

THE HOSPITAL OF SANTA CRUZ DE MENDOZA

If the façade of the Hospital of Tavera, with its simple forms, is an example of the more harsh and rigurous face of the Spanish Renaissance, the front of the Hospital of Santa Cruz is, on the contrary, a baroque and tender demonstration of Spain's lavish treasury of those years. An early example of that style that has been called plateresque, the façade of Santa Cruz has a particular infantile charm. All of those figures and Grecian diminutive forms that fuse on the columns and on the windows, in the shrine and in the curves of the arches, have something reminiscent of a "sacred history told with great simplicity", a little missionary pedagogy or like an illustrated edition of the Bible. One would not be able to say up to what point the discovery of America, with its indigenous baroque architecture, influenced in its turn colonial art, heavy, sylvan. The same historic trance gave rise in Portugal to a parallel style of our plateresque art: the Manueline. This concession to detail appears in all corners of the Hospital of Santa Cruz. Its planes are due to the imagination of the architect Enrique Egas. Aside from the books of the magnificent Provincial Library, the

The main staircase of the Hospital de Santa Cruz displays the Renaissance style with all of its detail and its undoubtable fineness.

Hospital houses the Museum of Santa Cruz. Toledo is not essentially an archaeological city. Towns of less importance, villages or camping sites, that played a small and discrete rôle in history, probably afford greater archaeological wealth. The majority of Roman and Visigothic remains of old *Toletum* have been buried by the historical winds of misfortune, the winds that blow —untiringly, obstinately— over the compass point of death. The pieces that once were the great exhibition of Charles V have experienced a more fortunate destiny: the ivory Christ by Becerra, the popular *Christ of the Light,* the coat-of-arms covering called *Tanto Monta,* with the motto of the Catholic King and Queen... and, above all, the rich collection of letters and documents that keep the signature, seal or a memory of the emperor. The exhibition of paintings does not lag behind in terms of what we have been able to admire in the Hospital de Tavera: Bassano, Tristan... and the inevitable El Greco; but in this abundant sampling of the moods and themes of the painter from Crete, a new view of his art: the *Asunción,* the work reflecting his death throes, the last utterance of his existence. «As in the eye of a needle —wrote Rilke on viewing it— I thread you with my longest contemplation while you ascend...»

The mixture of styles, so common in Toledo, is evident in the halls of the Taller del Moro: the arabesque motif of the wall juxtaposed with the Latin frieze of the ceiling.

The Taller del Moro, despite its humble name, is in every way a palace. This minutely and richly ornamented arch is proof of this.

The Alcázar of Toledo, built on the same hill where the fortress of Alfonso VI and the palace of Alfonso X were, was constructed during the reign of Carlos I. Alonso de Covarrubias directed the project and Villalpando, González de Lara and Juan de Herrera collaborated in its construction.

The monument to Carlos I enclosed by the elegant arches of the patio. The statue of the emperor is a reproduction of that carved by Leoni, which is now kept in Madrid.

QVEDARE
MVERTO
EN·AFRICA
O·ENTRARE
VENCEDOR
EN·TVNEZ

The Alcázar
of Toledo was
the scene of a
violent siege
during the
civil war of
1936. The
office of
Colonel
Moscardó,
who defended
the Alcázar,
manifests the
painful scars
of this episode
in Spain's
history. An
instructive
image of war
that demands
a heroic
tribute from
men of
honour.

Four great architects collaborated in drawing up the plans for the Alcázar: Alonso de Covarrubias, Francisco de Villalpando, Hernán González de Lara and Juan de Herrera. The Monument to Victory —dedicated to the heroes of the Alcázar— which stands opposite the western façade is the work of the sculptor Avalos.

The Alcázar was left almost completely in ruins after the siege and bombardment to which it was subjected by the Republican troops in 1936. The history of this monument is to a certain extent directly related to Spain's civil wars, considering that in 1710, during the War of Succession, it had been burned and destroyed.

CIVIL MONUMENTS

Monumentality occurs quite naturally in Toledo, quite appropriate to the historic events that took place in the town. One could say that the climate of Toledo, the very atmosphere, nourishes the buildings, makes them pack together, and converts them into palaces or monumets. History, that generous history that chose the streets of Toledo to enact its scenes, takes care to immediately inhabit them. In any house, in any corner, this sense of monumentality has shown itself already or can occur tomorrow. In any house the hand of the artist has come to rest to surprise us with a detail in good taste or an Arabesque made of sheer inspiration. Under any window the herald can be seen with a piece of history written on its shield. When we speak of monuments in Toledo we must confront the sad fact that we can only touch upon a few of the many that there are.

TOWNHALL

Although the primitive work of the Townhall dates from the reign of the Catholic King and Queen, and was ordered to be built by the magistrate Gómez Manrique under the guidance of Juan de Herrera, there is today scarcely a trace of those vestiges. The present structure is the work of Jorge Manuel Theotocopuli, the son of El Greco. Toledo's

The elegant façade of the Archbishop's Palace.

In the construction of the Town Hall of Toledo —a tribute to balance and harmony— Jorge Manuel Theotocopuli, the son of El Greco, played an important part. He finished and gave form to Herrera's original plan.

The empress Isabel lived and died in the palace of the Counts of Fuensalida; she was the wife of Carlos I. The door of the palace, decorated with blazons, is an attractive example of Gothic architecture.

Townhall could well illustrate that lesson of physics in which balance is transformed into beauty, that point where counterweight is coverted into harmony, and even the simple scribble of the number attains an esthetic posture. Toledo's Townhall conforms perfectly to the verses that Gómez Manrique composed concerning the art of governing, and that can be read on its staircase: "Noble, refined men who would rule Toledo... God gave you pillars upon which perch a rich roof; be firm and just."

PALACES OF FUENSALIDA AND OF LA AUDIENCIA: The enchantment of the portals.

Of all of the portals in Toledo —and they are many and varied— there exist two that have a joyful and charming likeness: the door of Fuensalida and that of la Audiencia.

The door of this latter is more ornate but nonetheless preserves the prestige of having seen pass through it with life and for the first time, the emperess Isabel, wife of Charles V, who died in the palace.

CASTLE OF SAN SERVANDO

The fortress of San Servando, that unfolds its troop of merlons before the bridge of Alcántara, was one of the pillars of defense of Toledo. Watchtower and barrier for the river Tajo, the castle of San Servando was built by Alphonso VI in commemoration of the battle of Badajoz and of the exemplary punishment that the Moors received in this thrust.

RAILROAD STATION

The railroad, that ingenious gust of imagination, that king of iron rails, was the pride of the industrial revolution in the last century. Almost all of the old stations in the world were built as if they were paying homage to bolts and iron. Toledo, however, by virtue of its history, didn't want to house the train —and its brave fans— in an iron cage. The city accepted the new invention in an Arabic palace, a sort of harem setting from the tale of a thousand and one nights.

The railway station, built in a picturesque Mudejar style, is the work of the architect Narciso Clavería.

The street of San Román exemplifies the twisting and tortuous nature of the old streets of Toledo.

The square of Zocodover is the pulse and heart of Toledo; the legendary and tumultuous timepiece of Toledo's life.

STREETS AND SQUARES OF OLD TOLEDO

Walks and moments of meditation are in Toledo two activities that are really one and the same, inseparable. The traveller walking through Toledo, perhaps lost, has the sensation that each of his senses' impressions escapes his consciousness; here he contemplates an iron grating, there he receives a fresh whif of orange blossoms or jasmine. Without knowing how he would feel, happy here and sad there, philosophical in one corner and down-trodden in another. This is one of the most suggestive mysteries of Toledo: the manner in which it works its way into our conscience, paralyzes us with its gaze, brushes up against us with its perfume, and leaves us later with our heart filled with a melancholy philosophy. "You must believe me, that this is possible —writes Rilke, excited, to a lady friend— that this exists; you must believe me, just like that." Obviously, it would be an error to stroll through Toledo following an itinerary. A schedule can be adhered to for visiting churches, monuments, or museums, but later on, if one wishes to

The poetry of the streets winding uphill at times expresses itself, for example in Calle de Moreto, with the use of classical and measured steps.

know the true spirit of Toledo, it is necessary to lose one's way. One has to get lost, "just like that".

The names of the streets are not important. Sometimes not even the façades of the houses are important. It is sufficient to be overtaken —extremely confused— by the atmosphere and the countryside. El Greco and Rilke saw Toledo with angels in the sky. El Greco and Rilke had been undoubtedly tainted by the magic wind of these ochre streets, these anguished little squares, of this prison, this patio.

We will come upon the square of Zocodover a thousand times because there is no detour in Toledo that doesn't lead us to this corner of the town. It's the market place and the centre of Toledo. Zocodover, with the moving about of its agora and the continuous murmur of its porticoes, is the theatre, stage, and the orchestra pit of Toledo. The city's life begins or ends somehow in this square. The traveller couldn't find a better spot from which to view the human secrets hidden in the town.

The Jewish quarter, while not what it used to be, has regained some of its commercial activity through tourism. The shops in this sector of the city are a paradise of souvenirs, an inevitable part of the tourist's programme.

The Mudejar tower of Santo Tomé looks over the street of the same name. The configuration of Toledo's streets could also be determined from the sky by observing the patterns traced by towers and belfries.

Following any of the almost infinite roads that lead away from Zocodover, perhaps the street of Comercio —that, faithful to its name— leads the traveller into the oldest quarter of the town, into the corners where the history of the city is slowly consumed. Toledo —as already said— is an introverted city, a town that hides itself in its lining like a chryspsalis in its cocoon. For this reason the patio, that divine invention of Latin civilization, that geometric fiesta of architecture, has a unique air in Toledo. Patios in Toledo aren't colourful and flowery as they are in Andalusia, but diaphanous and pensive. The gratings in Toledo are not welcoming, like their Andalusain brothers, to a confidential and chance conversation; they are more hermetic, more intimate. The traveller, upon stepping out onto a patio in Toledo, senses a desire to abandon himself to this play of gratings and prisons, and follow his footsteps to where he believes to have noticed a plaintive smell of jasmine.

> *Jasmine is an impoverished*
> *lover*
> *that lets his arms droop*
> *over the gratings.*

In the peaceful street of Santo Tomé, the traveller can make out perfectly the delicate Mudéjar tower of the church. Time is of no account. On the balcony of a nearby square white linen is hung out to dry in the sun. There is some-

The walls are the old stone defense of Toledo in the same way that the Tajo is the flowing and natural defense of the city. Only the bridges and gates break the ring of water and stone.

Toledo is a city of contrasts; sometimes introverted and secluded, shrouded in the ochre silence of narrow streets; other times open to the wideness and spaciousness of the plains; now and again hidden behind solid barred façades, and at times open to reveal the grace and arabesque design of its houses.

thing of a bell or incense in the rhythm of the sheets that sway in the breeze, something faintly reminiscent of freedom. But the traveller now works his way into the streets of the old Jewish quarter, streets that always end in the wall of misfortune. Once again the closed shutters, the curbstones of the well, the iron street lamps that cut the air. Once again that Jewish Toledo that folds around itself and keeps the confession of its soul contained with its walls. This is the street of the Jacintos, where don Diego de Sandoval fell in love with the Jewess Salomé; that is the house of Duende that burned on

Railings are an essential part of Toledo; they provide the town with an iron cloak which is also tender and dreamy in its twists and turns.

the night when God punished the witches that practised their crafts; that other is the tiny street of the Bitter Well were Rachel threw herself down believing that she saw the face of her lover at the bottom. All of Toledo is peopled with incredible histories, beautiful histories derived from the imagination. It could be said that the people of Toledo, conscious of this enormous, heavy dream that History could provoke in the streets, have sprinkled a little magic in the form of legends so that happenings are more human, more akin to our status. In this way, the History of Jewish presence in Toledo is firmly fixed in our memory. The Jewish presence is so ancient that even in the first Visigoth counsels the Hebrews were cited. They then lived in their hut-like dwellings lit with oil candles, where the city spills into the Tajo. In the heart of this ancient Jewish quarter lived the Hebrew Isaac

who safekept the jewels of Isabel the Catholic that were pawned and contributed to meeting the expenses related to the discovery of America. Cervantes and Mateo Alemán comment admiringly on the state of animation of the Alcaná, the most divergent commercial street in the Jewish quarter. There, as the chroniclers of the times wrote, could be found everything: jewels from Persia and Bagdad, fabrics from Damascus, shawls from Cachemira, silks from China, leather and repoussé work from Córdoba, ceramics from the Baleares, cloths from Segovia and Cuenca... The Alcaná was something like that fabulous medieval market that we can still find today in the Square of Jemaa of Marraquesch, with its charlatans and blind chanters, with its pickpockets, tooth sayers and magicians. But the Alcaná has disappeared, as the palace of Samuel Leví also vanished, which extended,

The patio is not an Arabic invention but a Roman one; however, the Arabs knew how to adorn it and adapt it to their architecture. Toledo's patios are a perfect manifestation of this mixture of Latin and Arabic elements, a frequent union in Toledo.

With so much historic stone, so much immortality in iron and brickwork, the ephemeral figure of the rose becomes almost human. Toledo is beyond time, but its gardens are a humble concession to Nature's seasons, a miniature monument to short-lived things.

from south to east of the synagogue. This living quarters, famous for its richness throughout the country, was located exactly in the area occupied today by the museum of El Greco, in the quarter where the marquis of Villena practised his art of alchemist and cook.

> *...this rest will I bear though should I die:*
> *that each day you would sing my death,*
> *those of the Tajo on her banks.*

Now the verses of Garcilaso come to mind. The traveller stands before the house where the poet was born; but the syllables of each verse mix with the sound of a bell, with the tumult of children playing, with the nay of a mule that doesn't want to move uphill... The traveller returns to the square of Zocodover and sits down to rest in a café. But the sun already begins to set and this is the prime hour in Toledo. Because Toledo, like Venice, like Istambul, is one of those cities that enjoy a personal and particular twilight. Its ochre colours turn golden when the sun starts its descent towards the horizon.

THE CIGARRALES: Last look at Toledo and the Tajo.

From the highway that follows the Tajo, all of Toledo can be seen: the bridges, walls, towers... The traveller, while dusk plants oranges on the countryside, remembers his first view of the town, when he thought he had discovered in the distance a stern and warlike city. From the top of the hill, that is off to the right, is to be seen a country estate sorrounded by cypress trees; to one side can be perceived a grove of ogive. They are the *cigarrales. The cigarral,* the stately house of Toledo, have a lazy, archaic twilight. Marañón felt in this spot a strange likeness between Toledo and the Mediterranean. The *cigarrales,* the final corner of Toledo where the cicadas hum a tune to the countryside and the soul, have overtones of a platonic, academic air and suggest strolls taken by philosophers. The *cigarrales* are an invitation to the two classical attitudes of wisdom: strolling and meditation. The traveller's feet are weary. But he can still meditate, on the edge of night, in the *cigarrales* of Toledo.

The cigarral, *the country house of Toledo, has the sunny serenity of rustic, Latin villas.*

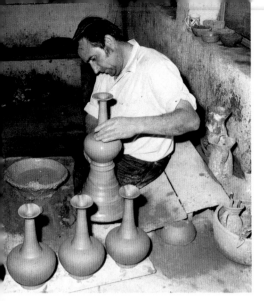

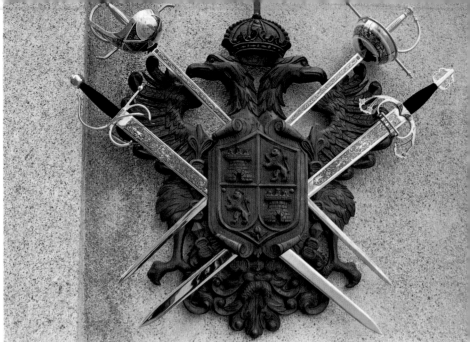

ARTISANRY AND FOLKLORE

Toledo is among those few cities of the world that have provided their local crafts with an international market. The same thing occurs with the artisanry of Toledo as with the Andalusian folklore: it has come to be identified with Spanish traits to the extent that Toledo has become Spain's most characteristic market for souvenirs. Because of a paradoxical whim of fate both the Andalusian song and Toledo's artisanry are products of a very local dedication, products of the soul or the imagination that develop

Toledo is one of the Spanish capitals boasting very characteristic artisan products. Ceramics, damaskeened steel, lace, the manufacture of swords... an endless repertory of small arts and crafts accumulated over the years. Perhaps the most representative of these arts is the manufacture of swords. The present sword factory in Toledo was founded in the XVIII century by Carlos III. It is probable that the chemical composition of the water of the Tajo influences the temper and quality of Toledo's swords.

in very specific geographical areas of the Iberian peninsula. Toledo manufactures everything: carpets, engravings, swords, figurines, dolls... And everything that Toledo makes is immediately converted into a classical ware. It is not in vane that Toledo has been for centuries a shop of artisans; the techniques of the distinct peoples that found a home in Toledo, have contributed to its artisanry affording a sense of the exotic and a sense of richness to the Germanic nature of its armory, Arabian influences found in swords and scabbards, African overtones in engravings and Asian touches in needlework... the artisanry of Toledo covers an endless array of wares. This same wealth of intentions, this same amplitude of influences, are to be found in Toledo's folklore. The typical costumes of the region are a festivity of colours and lace when they adorn the women, and they are elegant and somber when worn by the men. The music, inspired by picaresque and pastoral lyrics of the fifteenth and sixteenth centuries, is equally varied: From the *seguidilla* to the songs that are an authentic collection of sayings and popular philosophy. Finally, the *fiestas* are always ceremonious, because the people of Toledo are lovers of liturgy and rites; like all ancient towns, it has a ceremonial concept of happiness and sadness, a punctual calendar of its heart. The people are always ceremonious; whether attending, with luxury and pomp, the procession of the Corpus, or attending the Spring festival —remotely pagan— of the hunt. And we should not forget the *fiesta* of the bulls —so noteworthy in these lands, cradle of Lalanda, Ortega, Dominguín, etc.— which is essentially an ancestral rite.

Toledo's regional dress is wonderfully colourful and lavish, whether reference is made to the women working in the fields, the costumes of the Mancha, or those of the highlands. The apparel of Lagartera —a variation of the highland dress— is probably the most ostentatious of Spain's regional costumes.

Craftsmanship in ceramics also enjoys an old and noble tradition in Toledo. Numerous villages of the province compete in this industry.

GASTRONOMY

Owing to its geographical situation, between Old Castille, Extremadura, and the Mancha, Toledo offers us a varied gastronomy. The kitchen of Extremadura brings to the hearth of Toledo its hearty and country plates. But also across the Tajo reach Toledo the delicate and monkish arts with which Extremadura treats the cooking of small game. Toledo's Kitchen is essentially venatic, based upon the shotgun and the field: partridge, quail, and hare, animals that are quick on their feet and slow to cook; these constitute the basis of the region's gastronomy. The culinary art in Toledo, as all arts of the region, arises out of a series of influences that produce a savoury, gastronomic combination. The age-old Castillian kitchen, manly and patriarchal, contributes its mastery of roasts. The sacred alchemy is to be found in the magic blend and matching of this splendid union with the right wine. Toledo's wines (Esquivias, Lillo, Yepes, Cubas, Orgaz, Talavera, etc.), have a rich, hearty, and age-old taste, like its fame. And to top this off, sweets: those pastries with almonds, lightly Moorish to the point where they are baptized with wine, and they are given the name of *mazapán*.

Among Toledo's sweets special mention must be made to marzipan, directly related to Arabic confectionery recipes.

Toledo's cuisine is based for the most part on game. Stewed partridge and rabbit served with garlic are typical dishes.

TALAVERA DE LA REINA

Talavera, and again the Tajo river. Talavera, in the middle of those flat fields that sparkle in the sunshine with the colours of their ceramics: blue, ochre and yellow. From the name —*Lisbora or Talabrica*— that Talavera had in ancient times, there is no concrete data. Father Mariana, who was born in the village, believes that the royal denomination of Talavera comes from the Queen Juana Manuela, the wife of Henry II, who was overseer of the district. As is observed in the history of its baptism, Talavera is a town given artificial names, a town with a confused birth that grew, prodded along with the help of God, as the years swept by. Its image corresponds perfectly to its history: tattered canvasses, where living quarters were tacked on here and there, singular towers wedged between rooftops and chimneys, white façades with an endless stream of posters pasted between cables and balconies; *patios,* doors, and Visigoth wells in the midst of a labyrinth of shops and factories. Talavera, in addition to having a well-stocked market, is also the heart of Toledo's crafts and manufacturing, a hard-working shop of the province.

Talavera de la Reina is the centre of a rich district irrigated by the waters of the Tajo river. Famous for its artisan products, lace and ceramics, it is today an industrial town.

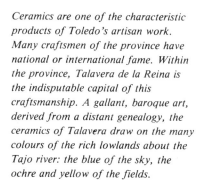

Ceramics are one of the characteristic products of Toledo's artisan work. Many craftsmen of the province have national or international fame. Within the province, Talavera de la Reina is the indisputable capital of this craftsmanship. A gallant, baroque art, derived from a distant genealogy, the ceramics of Talavera draw on the many colours of the rich lowlands about the Tajo river: the blue of the sky, the ochre and yellow of the fields.

But on the edge of this sympathetic bustle one can listen to the beating of Talavera's artisans' heart, steady and grave. A city of markets, it is also the snow-white and grumbling shop of fine lace. In the museum Ruiz de Luna the traveller can observe a notable sampling of Talavera's craftsmanship, especially those ceramics that have attained world fame since the sixteenth century. The objects pertinent to this work, decorated with themes of wildlife and local flower specimens, are exhibited today as veritable gems in all museums of the world. In the hermitage of Our Lady of the Prado, this labour reaches its apogee, its greatest decorative value. But Talavera is something more than its art. The Gothic collegiate church of Santa María, the church of Santiago, of Mudéjar origin, or the Romanesque temple of San Salvador, are only a part of its spirit.

To know and appreciate it, it's not enough to walk through the streets or to take in the façade of its churches; one must participate, although this would be with the eyes, in its essence: Beat with its pulse.

The mosaic, an inheritance of the decorative arts of the Moslems, is one of the most abundant ornamental elements in Toledo.

The colours of Toledo's countryside, the skies, the lands and the greenness of the plains along the Tajo, are reproduced in the diaphanous chromatics of the region's ceramics.

A night-time view of the bridge of San Martín at Toledo. ▷

Contents

That ancient part of history which is Spain is often referred to as "the bull's skin", because that is the shape of Spain on the map. The aim of this book is to present a detailed and comprehensive picture of a fragment of that "bull's skin", and to help this it includes a number of spectacular photographs. The Editor will be well satisfied if he has succeeded in giving you a deeper and better knowledge of Spain.

Collection ALL EUROPE

	Spanish	French	English	German	Italian	Catalan	Dutch	Swedish	Portuguese	Japanese	Arab
1 ANDORRA	■	■	■	■	■	□	■	□	□	□	□
2 LISBON	■	■	■	■	■	□	□	□	■	□	□
3 LONDON	■	■	■	■	■	□	□	□	□	■	□
4 BRUGES	■	■	■	■	□	□	■	□	□	□	□
5 PARIS	■	■	■	■	■	□	□	□	□	■	□
6 MONACO	■	■	■	■	■	□	□	□	□	□	□
7 VIENNA	■	■	■	■	■	□	■	□	□	■	■
8 NICE	■	■	■	■	■	□	□	□	□	□	□
9 CANNES	■	■	■	■	□	□	□	□	□	□	□
10 ROUSSILLON	■	■	■	■	□	■	□	□	□	□	□
11 VERDUN	■	■	■	■	□	□	□	□	□	□	□
12 THE TOWER OF LONDON	■	■	■	■	□	□	□	□	□	□	□
13 ANTWERP	■	■	■	■	□	□	■	□	□	□	□
14 WESTMINSTER ABBEY	■	■	■	■	□	□	□	□	□	□	□
15 THE SPANISH RIDING SCHOOL IN VIENNA	■	■	■	■	□	□	□	□	□	□	□
16 FATIMA	■	■	■	■	□	□	□	□	■	□	□
17 WINDSOR CASTLE	■	■	■	■	□	□	□	□	□	■	□
18 THE OPAL COAST	□	■	■	■	□	□	□	□	□	□	□
19 COTE D'AZUR	■	■	■	■	□	□	□	□	□	□	□
20 AUSTRIA	■	■	■	■	□	□	□	□	□	□	□
21 LOURDES	■	■	■	■	□	□	□	□	□	□	□
22 BRUSSELS	■	■	■	■	□	□	■	□	□	□	□

Collection ALL AMERICA

	Spanish	French	English	German	Italian	Catalan	Dutch	Swedish	Portuguese	Japanese	Arab
1 PUERTO RICO	■	□	■	□	□	□	□	□	□	□	□
2 SANTO DOMINGO	■	□	■	□	□	□	□	□	□	□	□

Collection ALL AFRICA

	Spanish	French	English	German	Italian	Catalan	Dutch	Swedish	Portuguese	Japanese	Arab
1 MOROCCO	■	■	■	■	□	□	□	□	□	□	■

Collection ART IN SPAIN

	Spanish	French	English	German	Italian	Catalan	Dutch	Swedish	Portuguese	Japanese	Arab
1 PALAU DE LA MUSICA CATALANA (Catalan Palace of Music)	■	■	■	■	□	■	□	□	□	□	□
2 GAUDI	■	■	■	■	■	□	□	□	□	□	□
3 PRADO MUSEUM I (Spanish Painting)	■	■	■	■	□	□	□	□	□	■	□
4 PRADO MUSEUM II (Foreign Painting)	■	■	■	■	□	□	□	□	□	□	□
5 THE ROOF-BOSSES OF THE CATHEDRAL OF GERONA	■	□	□	□	□	□	□	□	□	□	□
6 THE CASTLE OF XAVIER	■	■	■	■	□	□	□	□	□	□	□
7 THE ROMANESQUE STYLE IN SPAIN	■	■	■	□	□	□	□	□	□	□	□
8 SPANISH CASTLES	■	■	■	■	□	□	□	□	□	□	□
9 THE CATHEDRALS OF SPAIN	■	■	■	■	□	□	□	□	□	□	□
10 THE CATHEDRAL OF GERONA	■	■	■	■	□	□	□	□	□	□	□
11 GRAN TEATRO DEL LICEO DE BARCELONA (The Great Opera House)	■	■	■	■	■	■	□	□	□	□	□
12 THE ROMANESQUE STYLE IN CATALONIA	■	■	■	■	□	□	□	□	□	□	□
13 LA RIOJA: ART TREASURES AND WINE-GROWING RESOURCES	■	■	■	■	□	□	□	□	□	□	□
14 PICASSO	■	■	■	■	□	□	□	□	□	□	□
15 THE BAROQUE STYLE IN SPAIN	■	■	■	■	■	□	□	□	□	□	□
16 ROMAN REMAINS IN SPAIN	■	■	■	■	□	□	□	□	□	□	□
17 THE GOTHIC STYLE IN SPAIN	■	■	■	■	□	□	□	□	□	□	□
18 THE WINES OF CATALONIA	■	■	■	■	□	□	□	□	□	□	□
19 THE ALHAMBRA AND THE GENERALIFE	■	■	■	■	■	□	□	□	□	□	□
20 GRANADA AND THE ALHAMBRA (ARAB AND MAURESQUE MONUMENTS OF CORDOVA, SEVILLE AND GRANADA)	■	□	□	□	□	□	□	□	□	□	□

Collection ALL SPAIN

	Spanish	French	English	German	Italian	Catalan	Dutch	Swedish	Portuguese	Japanese	Arab
1 ALL MADRID	■	■	■	■	■	□	□	□	□	■	□
2 ALL BARCELONA	■	■	■	■	■	■	□	□	□	□	□
3 ALL SEVILLE	■	■	■	■	■	□	□	□	□	■	□
4 ALL MAJORCA	■	■	■	■	■	□	□	□	□	□	□
5 ALL THE COSTA BRAVA	■	■	■	■	■	□	□	□	□	□	□
6 ALL MALAGA and the Costa del Sol	■	■	■	■	■	□	□	□	□	□	□
7 ALL THE CANARY ISLANDS I, Lanzarote and Fuerteventura	■	■	■	■	□	□	■	■	□	□	□
8 ALL CORDOBA	■	■	■	■	■	□	□	□	□	□	□
9 ALL GRANADA	■	■	■	■	■	□	□	□	□	□	□
10 ALL VALENCIA	■	■	■	■	□	□	□	□	□	□	□
11 ALL TOLEDO	■	■	■	■	■	□	□	□	□	■	□
12 ALL SANTIAGO and the Rías Bajas	■	■	■	■	□	□	□	□	□	□	□
13 ALL IBIZA and Formentera	■	■	■	■	□	□	□	□	□	□	□
14 ALL CADIZ and the Costa de la Luz	■	■	■	■	□	□	□	□	□	□	□
15 ALL MONTSERRAT	■	■	■	■	□	□	□	□	□	□	□
16 ALL SANTANDER and the Costa Esmeralda	■	■	■	■	□	□	□	□	□	□	□
17 ALL THE CANARY ISLANDS II, Tenerife, La Palma, Gomera, Hierro	■	■	■	■	□	□	■	■	□	□	□
18 ALL PEÑISCOLA	■	■	■	■	□	□	□	□	□	□	□
19 ALL SITGES	■	■	■	■	□	□	□	□	□	□	□
20 ALL BURGOS, Covarrubias and Santo Domingo de Silos	■	■	■	■	□	□	□	□	□	□	□
21 ALL ALICANTE and the Costa Blanca	■	■	■	■	□	■	□	□	□	□	□
22 ALL NAVARRA	■	■	■	■	□	□	□	□	□	□	□
23 ALL LERIDA Province and Pyrenees	■	■	■	■	□	■	□	□	□	□	□
24 ALL SEGOVIA and Province	■	■	■	■	□	□	□	□	□	□	□
25 ALL SARAGOSSA and Province	■	■	■	■	□	□	□	□	□	□	□
26 ALL SALAMANCA and Province	■	■	■	■	□	□	□	□	■	□	□
27 ALL AVILA and Province	■	■	■	■	□	□	□	□	□	□	□
28 ALL MINORCA	■	■	■	■	□	□	□	□	□	□	□
29 ALL SAN SEBASTIAN and Province	■	■	■	■	□	□	□	□	□	□	□
30 ALL ASTURIAS	■	■	■	■	□	□	□	□	□	□	□
31 ALL CORUNNA and the Rías Altas	■	■	■	■	□	□	□	□	□	□	□
32 ALL TARRAGONA and Province	■	■	■	■	□	□	□	□	□	□	□
33 ALL MURCIA and Province	■	■	■	■	□	□	□	□	□	□	□
34 ALL VALLADOLID and Province	■	■	■	■	□	□	□	□	□	□	□
35 ALL GIRONA and Province	■	■	■	■	□	□	□	□	□	□	□
36 ALL HUESCA and Province	■	■	□	□	□	□	□	□	□	□	□
37 ALL JAEN and Province	■	■	■	■	□	□	□	□	□	□	□
38 ALL ALMERIA and Province	■	■	■	■	□	□	□	□	□	□	□
39 ALL CASTELLON and the Costa del Azahar	■	■	■	■	□	□	□	□	□	□	□
40 ALL CUENCA and Province	■	■	□	□	□	□	□	□	□	□	□
41 ALL LEON and Province	■	■	■	■	□	□	□	□	□	□	□
42 ALL PONTEVEDRA, VIGO and the Rías Bajas	■	■	■	■	□	□	□	□	□	□	□
43 ALL RONDA	■	■	■	■	□	□	□	□	□	□	□
44 ALL SORIA	■	■	■	■	□	□	□	□	□	□	□

The printing of this book was completed
in the workshops of FISA · Industrias
Gráficas, Palaudarias, 26 · Barcelona
(Spain)